Wool

Andrew Langley

Crabtree Publishing Company

www.crabtreebooks.com

Crabtree Publishing Company

www.crabtreebooks.com

All rights reserved.
Author: Andrew Langley
Editors: Annabel Savery, Adrianna Morganelli
Proofreaders: Michael Hodge, Crystal Sikkens
Project editor: Robert Walker
Designer: Ian Winton
Illustrator: Ian Winton
Picture researcher: Rachel Tisdale
Production coordinator: Margaret Amy Salter
Prepress technician: Margaret Amy Salter

© 2009 Crabtree Publishing Company

Acknowledgements: Australian Wool Innovation: 9, 10 top, 11. cfgphoto.com: 6 and 7 (Geff Bryant / Clare Selby). CFWImages: 8 (John R Kreul), 18 (Chris Fairclough). Discovery Picture Library: 5 (Chris Fairclough). GettyImages: cover main (Keren Su), 14 (Gabriela Hasbun). Icetrek.com: 16 (Eric Phillips). Istockphoto: head panels (Naci Yavuz), title page and 21 (Madeleine Openshaw), 4, 15 (Marie Cheek), 17 (Pali Rao), 19 (Karl Friedrich Hohl), 20. The British Wool Marketing Board: 10 bottom, 12, 13.

Library and Archives Canada Cataloguing in Publication

Langley, Andrew
    Wool / Andrew Langley.

(Everyday materials)
Includes index.
ISBN 978-0-7787-4131-2 (bound).--ISBN 978-0-7787-4138-1 (pbk.)

    1. Wool--Juvenile literature. I. Title. II. Series: Langley, Andrew.
Everday materials.

TS1547.L35 2008   j677'.31   C2008-903640-9

Library of Congress Cataloging-in-Publication Data

Langley, Andrew.
    Wool / Andrew Langley.
        p. cm. -- (Everyday materials)
    Includes index.
    ISBN-13: 978-0-7787-4138-1 (pbk. : alk. paper)
    ISBN-10: 0-7787-4138-9 (pbk. : alk. paper)
    ISBN-13: 978-0-7787-4131-2 (reinforced lib. binding : alk. paper)
    ISBN-10: 0-7787-4131-1 (reinforced lib. binding : alk. paper)
    1. Wool--Juvenile literature. I. Title. II. Series.

TS1547.L33 2009
677'.31--dc22

2008025323

Crabtree Publishing Company

www.crabtreebooks.com   1-800-387-7650

Published in Canada
Crabtree Publishing
616 Welland Ave.
St. Catharines, Ontario
L2M 5V6

Published in the United States
Crabtree Publishing
PMB16A
350 Fifth Ave., Suite 3308
New York, NY 10118

First published in 2008
by Wayland
338 Euston Road
London NW1 3BH

Wayland Australia
Level 17/207 Kent Street
Sydney, NSW 2000

Copyright © Wayland 2008

Contents

What is wool?   4

Where does wool come from?   6

Shearing the fleece   8

Cleaning   10

Making wool yarn   12

Making clothes   14

Special uses   16

Recycling wool   18

Quiz   20

Wool topic web   21

Glossary   22

Further information   23

Index   24

What is wool?

Wool is a natural material. It is a **fiber** that grows just like hair. Wool grows on sheep and some other animals.

4

Wool is soft and springy to touch. It can be made into rugs, blankets, and cloth. Woolen clothes keep us warm in cold weather.

Eye spy

Do you have any woolen clothes? Look for a label that says "pure wool."

Where does wool come from?

Nearly all wool comes from sheep. A sheep grows a thick coat of wool all over its body. This coat is called a **fleece**.

6

A few other animals have fleece coats. Some goats grow long and soft wool coats. Farmers also keep **alpacas** and **llamas** for their wool.

Llamas

Shearing the fleece

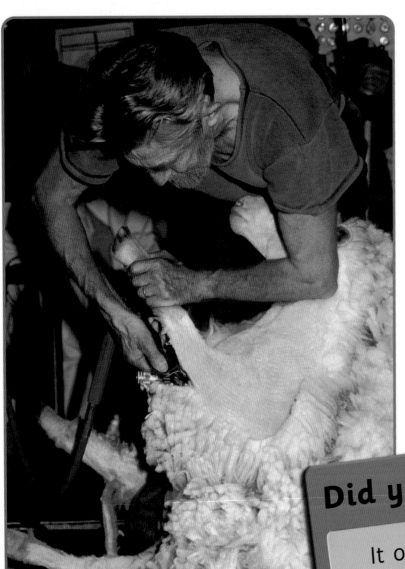

In summer, workers cut the wool off the sheep. This is called **shearing**. The fleece is cut off in a single piece. It does not hurt.

Did you know?

It only takes four minutes for an expert shearer to shear one sheep.

A worker looks at each fleece carefully. Patches of thin or dirty wool are cut out. Then the fleeces are packed in bundles called **bales**.

Cleaning

Fleeces are often dirty with thorns and mud from the fields. They contain a natural grease called **lanolin**. Lanolin makes the fleece **waterproof**. The fleeces need to be sorted before they can be used.

At the factory, the wool goes through a series of soapy baths. These wash out the dirt and the lanolin.

Did you know?

Lanolin is not thrown away. It is cleaned and made into shampoo and soap.

11

Making wool yarn

The clean wool passes through
special rollers. These have tiny wire
teeth. The teeth comb the fibers so
they all lie the same way.

The wool is divided into strips. Machines spin and pull the wool strips. This turns the fibers into a thread called **yarn**.

Eye spy

Take some yarn from an old woolen sock or scarf. If you untwist it, the yarn will come apart. You can see the wool fibers.

Here, wool yarn is being spun onto reels.

Making clothes

A machine called a **loom** makes the yarn into woolen cloth. The yarn is stretched across the loom. The loom **weaves** another thread of yarn in between these threads. It goes back and forth hundreds of times. This makes a piece of cloth.

To make clothes, **laser machines** cut shapes out of woolen cloth. Another machine **stitches** the pieces together with cotton thread. Some clothes are stitched together by hand.

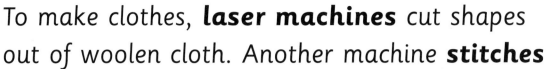

Did you know?

Do you know anyone who knits with wool? They use special needles to weave the wool into cloth.

Special uses

Wool keeps us warm and cozy. People who go to very cold places, such as **astronauts** and **polar travelers**, wear special wool clothes.

Wool is used in some unusual places. The covering on a tennis ball and the tip of a felt-tip pen are both made of wool.

What do you think?

Find something made of woolen cloth. Find another made of **polyester** (look on the labels). Do they feel different?

Recycling wool

We will never run out of wool. There are millions of sheep and other wooly animals in the world. They will always grow new fleeces.

We can use wool again. At special recycling plants, workers take apart old wool clothes. The fibers are spun into new yarn to make new clothes.

Old yarn can be used again to make new clothes.

Quiz

Questions

1. What kind of animal does most wool come from?

2. What does a shearer do?

3. What do we call the natural grease in wool?

4. What is wool thread called?

5. What kind of machine is a loom?

Answers

5. A loom is a machine for weaving cloth.

4. Wool thread is called yarn.

3. Natural grease in wool is called lanolin.

2. A shearer cuts the fleece from a sheep.

1. Most wool comes from sheep.

Wool topic web

Art and design
You can try knitting with wool to make cloth. Ask an adult to show you how. You will need special knitting needles and some wool.

English
Some famous stories have been written about wool. The most famous is the Greek legend of Jason and his search for the Golden Fleece.

History
The Romans set up the first wool factory in England. English people were already using wool to make clothes, but the factory made the process quicker.

Geography
The biggest wool-making countries are Australia, China, and New Zealand.

Science
Wool is waterproof. Water drops roll off it instead of soaking into it. What other materials are waterproof?

Glossary

alpaca An animal from South America that grows long wooly hair

astronaut A space traveler

bale A bundle of material tied together

fiber A thin strand or thread of material

fleece The whole wool coat of a sheep

lanolin The natural oil or grease produced by a sheep

laser machine A machine that uses a very powerful beam of light to cut material

llama An animal (from the camel family) that grows wool

loom A machine for weaving cloth

polar traveler Someone who travels in the very cold regions of the North Pole or the South Pole

polyester A kind of plastic used to make thread or cloth

shearing Cutting off the fleece from a sheep, using clippers

stitch To join one piece of material to another with loops of thread

waterproof Describes a material that water cannot get through

weave To make cloth by lacing together threads of yarn; one set of threads goes top to bottom, and the other goes side to side

yarn Thin thread made by spinning strands of wool fiber together

Further information

Books to read

Find Out About: Find Out About Wool and Fibre. Henry Pluckrose.
    Franklin Watts Ltd., 2002.

Raintree Perspectives: Using Materials: How We Use Wool. Chris Oxlade. Raintree
    Publishers, 2004.

Start-Up Science: Materials. Claire Llewellyn. Evans Brothers Ltd., 2004.

Websites to visit

BBC Schools
http://www.bbc.co.uk/schools/scienceclips/ages/5_6/sorting_using_mate.shtml
Learn all about different types of materials and their properties.

Recycling guide
http://www.recycling-guide.org.uk/textiles.html
Learn all about how we can recycle clothes.

UK Agriculture
http://www.ukagriculture.com/fun_and_games/sheep_game.cfm
You can play this fun game and then have a look around the website to learn more about sheep and wool.

Index

alpacas 7

astronauts 16

bales 9

blankets 5

cloth 5, 14, 15, 17, 20, 21

clothes 5, 14, 15, 16, 19, 21

comb 12

cotton 15

felt-tip pen 17

fiber 4, 12, 13, 19

fleece 6, 7, 8, 9, 10, 18, 20, 21

goats 7

knit 15, 21

lanolin 10, 11, 20

laser machines 15

llamas 7

loom 14, 20

natural material 4

needles 15, 21

New Zealand 19, 21

polar travelers 16

polyester 17

rabbit 7

recycling 18, 19

rollers 12

rugs 5

shearer 8, 20

sheep 4, 6, 8, 18, 19, 20

stitch 15

tennis ball 17

thread 13, 15, 20

waterproof 10, 21

weaving 14, 15, 20

yarn 12, 13, 14, 19, 20

Printed in China